# Human-Computer Interaction
## By Solis Tech

# The Fundamentals Made Easy!

## 2nd Edition

**Human-Computer Interaction (2nd Edition) :** The Fundamentals Made Easy!

# Table of Contents

Introduction........................................................................................4

Chapter 1 - Aspects of HCI.................................................................5

Chapter 2 - The Human Side in the HCI..........................................8

Chapter 3 - The Computer Side in the HCI...................................27

Conclusion........................................................................................42

# Introduction

I want to thank you and congratulate you for purchasing the book, "Human-Computer Interaction: The Fundamentals Made Easy!"

This book contains proven steps and strategies on how to conceptualize and design a computer system that incorporate principles on effective interaction between the user and the device.

Human-computer interaction (HCI) is the study of the interaction between people and computers and the degree at which computers are developed enough to successfully interact with humans. So many institutions particularly academic and corporations now study HCI. Unfortunately, ease-of-use has not been a priority to most computer systems developer. The issue continues to bedevil the HCI community as accusations still abound that computer makers are still indifferent and are not making enough effort to make truly user-friendly products.

On the other hand, the designing task of computer system developers is not simple either as computers are very complex products. It is also true that the demand for use of computers have grown by leaps and bounds outstripping the need for ease-of-use by a significant margin. If you are a computer designer or simply have basic interest in making devices more effective for users, this book will help you a lot.

Thanks again for purchasing this book, I hope you enjoy it!

# Chapter 1: Aspects of HCI

## Main aspects of HCI

HCI is composed of three main features, namely: the user, the computer, and their interaction or how they work together.

"User" refers to either the individual or the group of users doing things together. An understanding of how the people's sense of sight, hearing, and touch send information is very important. Also, the type of mental models of interactions differs according to the personality of the user. And finally, interactions are also influenced by cultural and national differences.

"Computer," on the other hand, pertains to all technology from desktop to huge computer systems. As an example, if the topic is website design, the computer would then be the website. "Computers" would also include gadgets like mobile phones or even VCRs.

Finally, the "Interaction" is what happens as "User" uses the "Computer" to achieve a certain objective. Humans, of course, are totally different from machines. So the HCI's main intent is to ensure a successful interaction between the two.

In this aspect, adequate knowledge about humans and computers are critical to realize a functioning system. You need to seek inputs from users. Such knowledge would provide much needed information in determining schedule and budget that are crucial to the systems. In effect there are ideal situations and perfect systems. But the key is finding the balance between what is ideal and what is really feasible given the existing situation.

## Objectives of HCI

HCI aims to come up with systems that are functional, usable, and safe. Developing computer systems with excellent usability depends on:

- having enough understanding of the aspects that lead people to use technology in certain ways
- being able to devise tools and ways for creating suitable systems
- the development of safe, effective, and efficient interaction
- making people the priority

The main philosophy underneath HCI is that the users or the people using the computers always come first. Developers must always be guided by the users' needs and preferences in designing systems. It is the system that should match the requirements of human users and not people changing to suit the nature of the machines.

## The primacy of usability

Usability is one of the principal considerations in HCI. It is simply about ensuring that a system can be easily learned and used or be what is called user-friendly. A system is considered usable if it:

- can be learned easily
- can be remembered easily in terms of use
- is effective
- is efficient
- is safe
- is enjoyable

Lack of usability means wasted time, mistakes, and disappointments. Unfortunately, a lot of existing systems and devices have been designed without sufficient attention to usability. These include ATM, the Web, computer, printer, mobile phone, personal organizer, coffee machine, remote control, soft drink machine, ticket machine, photocopier, stereo, watch, video game, library information systems, and calculator.

A good example is the photocopier. If you are not familiar with the symbols on the buttons you will be greatly confused. For instance, the big button with the C on it actually refers to Clear, not Copy. The button used to produce copies is actually on the left side with an unrelated symbol. Devices and gadgets should be easy, effortless, and enjoyable to use.

Analyzing and designing a system based on HCI principles involve a lot of factors that produce really complex analysis because of interactions among many of them. The major factors are:

1. The User – motivation, satisfaction, experience, enjoyment, personality. Also cognitive processes and capabilities

2. User Interface – navigation, output devices, icons, commands, input devices, graphics, dialogue structures, user support, use of color, multimedia, natural language

3. Environmental Factors – health and safety, noise, heating, lighting, ventilation

4. Organization Factors – job design, work organization, training, roles, politics

5. Task Factors – task allocation, skills, easy, novel, complex, monitoring

6. Comfort Factors – seating, layout, equipment

7. Constraints – budgets, buildings, cost, equipment, timescales, staff
8. Productivity Factors – decrease costs, increase quality, increase innovation, increase output, decrease errors
9. System Functionality – software, hardware, application

There are different disciplines representing a wide array of subjects that are covered in HCI. The manifold inputs from these fields have continued to enrich HCI. The disciplines include:

- Cognitive Psychology – limitations, performance predictions, information processing, cooperative working, capabilities
- Ergonomics – display readability, hardware design
- Computer Science – graphics, software design, prototyping tools, technology, User Interface Management Systems (UIMS) and User Interface Development Environments (UIDE)
- Social Psychology – social and organizational structures
- Engineering and Design – engineering principles, graphic designs
- Linguistics – natural language interfaces
- Philosophy, Sociology, and Anthropology – computer supported cooperative work (CSCW)
- Artificial Intelligence – intelligent software

# Chapter 2: The Human Side in the HCI

Some of the key aspects that shed light on the human side of HCI are:

1. <u>Perceptual-Motor Interaction</u>. Effective human-computer interface design requires an appreciation of the whole human perceptual-motor system. The information-processing approach is central to the perceptual-motor behavior study and for considering the human factors in HCI. An effective interface design reflects the designer's knowledge of the perceptual such as visual displays, use of sound, and graphics. Also the cognitive exemplified by conceptual models and desktop metaphors as well as motoric constraints like ergonomic keyboards of the human perpetual-motor system.

   Man has gone beyond the use of computer punch cards and command-line interfaces. We now use speech recognition, eye-gaze control, and graphical user interfaces. The importance of various perceptual, cognitive, and motor constraints of the human system is now better recognized in HCI. An effective interface must take into account the perceptual and action expectations of users, the action that is seen with a response location, and the mapping of the perceptual-motor workspaces.

## Perceptual motor behavior

For many enthusiasts in perceptual-motor behavior, the framework on information processing has always been a source of key empirical and theoretical ideas. The perceptual-motor behavior study includes motor learning processes, information needs of motor set-up, and memory capacity in motors. This concept that uses information processing identifies man as a major information processor in the level of complex computing. Analyzing via information processing involves using encoded perceptual information in assessing behavior, the way the information is used by psychological subsystems, and how these subsystems are organized in terms of functions.

One key principle relevant to HCI in human information processing is the focus on cognitive steps prior to action. The action is simply the outcome of the string of intricate information processing activities. Of particular concern is the time involved in engaging a target. In the field of HCI, this aspect has provided the operational designs for the computer mouse, for instance. Based on error and speed measures, cursor positioning and movement have been refined. It has also used Fitts' law in predicting the time at which the target is engaged. It incorporates the reality that pointing devices are reliant on the movement of hands.

Fitts' law states that pointing time is a function of the width to distance characteristic of the target. Meaning, to ensure a level of accuracy, time of

8

movement should increase as the movement's distance lengthens or the target's width shrinks. Currently, this principle is used in testing pointing devices though it has significant limitations. One is that other than target size and distance, it does not indicate other factors that impact target time. There are actually many possible targets present in most HCI environments. The impact of these stimuli coming from unintended targets can be substantial.

Another principle, the HickHyman law, forecasts the length of time a decision is made to choose a response out of many potential responses to the target. The decision time grows with the increase in the number of possible responses. Combined, Fitts and HickHyman laws provide a better basis for predicting outcome. As HCI situations in the area of perceptual-motor interfaces become more complex, indexing through time will no longer be sufficient. This is true with such newer interfaces like gestural, augmented reality, haptic, and teleoperation where interactions are more dynamic.

Researchers have thus pushed for additional framework, the movement process approach, to complement the time-based analysis. The resulting synthesis is that apart from the preceding activities of an action or movement, the movement itself must also be considered. This led to the study of a movement's kinematics to understand its organization and control.

2. <u>Human Information Processing.</u> Aspects of human information processing such as models, theories, and methods are currently well developed. The available knowhow in this field is broadly useful to HCI in general such as in the representation and communication of knowledge and visual display design. An effective HCI requires making the interaction compatible with the human information-processing capabilities. Many things about human information processing have been integrated into cognitive architectures that are now applicable to HCI. These applications include the Model Human Processor, the Act model, the SOAR model, and the Epic model.

**Information processing methods**

Researchers are increasingly using behavioral methods that are time-based and with psychophysiological orientation. Signal detection is one of the most effective methods for the study of information processing. This strategy includes classifying certain events as a signal and then detecting if the signal is present. "Noise trials" are those trials that do not show the presence of the signal. "Hit rate" refers to the fraction of trials where the signal was detected. "False alarm rate" is the fraction of trials where the signal was not present. The combination of these alarm rates enables the evaluation of bias. During trials, the conclusion of whether information deserves a signal depends on the presented information. Both signal and noise trials constitute distribution of probability. A decision is made for each trial that says an event is from noise or signal distribution.

9

Based on a certain standard, a subject may indicate if signal is absent or present. Numerous measures of bias and detectability exist depending on applicable theories and assumptions. The analyses of signal detection are very useful because it is applicable to any binary-structured task. For instance, the words coming from a memory task can be classified as a hit rate or false alarm depending on the accuracy of detection. Researchers use the analysis result to know if variables are determining the detection of an item as a response or simply old bias. Signal detection methodology has been widely utilized in vigilance research. Changes are monitored in vigilance tasks through a display monitor. These tasks are present in computer-related undertakings like operations monitoring for computer networks.

## Alternate methodologies/ recent developments

Apart from the human information processing method, other approaches were considered. The information processing approach has been relatively successful, however, in providing remedies on theoretical and applied levels compared to other methodologies. Some of these alternate approaches are:

Ecological approach

The emphasis here is on the analysis of data from the optic line up and the interaction among these data vis-a-vis what is happening in the environment. Perception is highlighted while discounting cognitive processes and mental depiction. HCI, however, mainly dwells on the performance of information-heavy tasks in a non-natural, artificial environment. Internet-based information schemes, for instance, is mainly about information processing. If it is consistent with information processing trials, it could be very useful for relevant task analyses. In HCI, knowing better the data that an observer has in a simulated environment is very important with ecologically-relevant tasks. Recent studies, for example, in the field of aviation have emphasized information analysis in the flight environment. These ecological analyses are important and need to be assimilated in the information-processing framework.

Chronometric methods

The chronometric approach has time as its most important factor in information processing studies. Specifically, the reaction time or RT is the number one dependent variable in the approach. RT is the most dominant among all measures in use because of the high level analysis techniques developed for it and its level of sensitivity. One technique used in determining the length of time of a processing stage is the "subtractive method." The time is determined by simply subtracting from the RT of a harder task the RT of an easier one. Processes where the subtractive method is used include memory search and rotation rates of the mind.

### Cybernetic approach

Cybernetic, on the other hand, is similar to ecological approach although more importance is placed on self-regulation in controlling cognition and insight. Cognition happens when sensory reaction is under motor control. This approach has some basic differences vis-a-vis information processing. One is in the area of behavioral cybernetics. Through motor-sensory behavior, the information feedback mechanism is actively controlled while the information processing has no such feature. This feature stems from the perception of motor behavior as having no principal role in the organization or information control. As an example, in the HCI involving a driver and his vehicle, information processing is key to understanding their interaction based on cognition using computers.

### Cognitive neuroscience

This is a fast expanding field. Its main research focus is to study the mechanisms of the brain that pertain to cognition. Behavioral studies in information processing supplies much of the basis for this field. The ultimate aim is to bridge the gap between brain activity and the processing of information.

### Situated Cognition

Also recently pushed is another method called situated cognition. In this concept, most of the information processing happens outside the individual and guided by external reality. The focus is on analyzing the environment specifically the constraints and its background. An empirical issue is how much the principles generated by information processing studies cover other aspects.

### Speed-Accuracy Approach

Otherwise called "speed-accuracy tradeoff," it concerns the speed of response to accuracy. The slower the response, the more accurate is the result and vice versa. One consequence of higher accuracy is that a big reduction in response time (RT) will result with just a little increase in errors. Accuracy and speed need to be studied and measured. For instance in typing, if one is less concerned with accuracy more texts can be entered in a faster way. This approach, however, can be more promising than RT researches in the sense that potentially more information will be available about the effect of variables on intercept. So the speed accuracy method is more often applied in situations that deal heavily with the speed accuracy aspect.

Neuroimaging and psychophysiological approach

The faster the response the lower the accuracy. This aspect concerns event-related potentials or ERPs. ERP refers to brain activity changes triggered by certain events like the advent of a stimulus. It has the following features: the first negative (N1), first positive (P1), and the post perceptual or P3. The most extensively studied feature is the P3. It was applied in an HCI study involving playing the game Tetris, programming, and text editing using the paper/pencil medium for comparison. The results suggest more cognitive resources lost and increased feeling of fatigue due to HCI tasks than by paper/pencil. Still, another method is the lateralized readiness potential or LRP which is a measure of how the right and left sides of the brain differ from each other in terms of activity.

3.  Mental Models in Human–Computer Interaction.  Studying mental models can help understand HCI by inspecting the processes by which such models impact behavior. For example, mental models of machines can enable both novice and seasoned problem solvers to find new methods for fulfilling a task through more elaborate encoding of remembered methods.

The Reverse Polish Notation is a great example of this. There is also a general theory that says readers develop a representation in their mind at several levels of what they read. First is the encoding of text, followed by the representation of propositional content of text.  Finally, to this text, they integrate world knowledge to form a mental model of the situation described.

Readers also have the ability to look for ideas in multiple texts. They construct a kind of structured mental maps that show which documents contained which ideas even when they did not expect to need it while reading. Mental models are generally considered as semantic knowledge. Focusing on the degree of commonality among team members, for instance, when it comes to knowledge and beliefs, allows quantitative measures of similarity and differences which is the language of computers.

**Mental models of texts and other artifacts**

The main idea here is that readers form mental representations at various levels of what they read. They first do the encoding of the syntax and words of the text. Then they make the proposed context representation of the text. Lastly, they make the intended context representation and the described situation's mental model. Studies show that people construct mental models within the shared location or its representation organizing long term memory recoveries based on the mental models. Doing this in multiple locations is next to impossible. But what all the studies prove is that readers suddenly form a mental representation farther than the very text including its meaning when trying to understand it. They even use extrapolations to make a situation model. Existing text comprehension data point to the idea that a representation of what an artifact stands for pretty much describes a mental model.

Those findings about mental models have practical applications in designing HCI instructions and interfaces. Take for example the calculator stack and the copy buffer. Theoretical instructions should be formulated to remedy the discrepancy because current interfaces do not allow enough space for a device. A user interface redesign is needed for a visible device space. Text comprehension is so relevant to HCI because HCI is mainly reading text. Of direct relevance to design in HCI are the following important issues: a) the way in which readers exploit many texts of one topic; and b) usability when it comes to documents which combine text and multiple media.

## Mental model instructions

The following are principles in designing instructional multimedia materials:

- Multiple presentation

  This pertains to the principle that a combination of text and pictorial explanations is more effective than words alone. Without pictures, forming a good mental image is difficult thereby hindering the learning process. This was validated by a study that compared four situations namely: pictures only, words plus pictures, words only, and control. The group that used pictures and words produced the most number of creative solutions to a problem. It is no surprise that animation that offers no narration was considered lacking in instructional value. Studies tend to convincingly support this observation.

- Contiguity principle

  This posits that it is more effective to have a simultaneous presentation of verbal and visual materials instead of one after another as it would enable learners to establish connections that can refer to others. An example is a study of how a bicycle pump operates using computer animation. Two versions were compared wherein one had both pictures and words while the other version had words only before showing the pictures. Both incorporated tests for creativity in problem solving. The group that used the combined words and pictures produced solutions 50% more than the other version.

- Individual differences principle

This principle maintains that aspects like previous knowledge will enhance a learning activity that uses multimedia materials. Experienced learners will have fewer problems with a successive narration-animation presentation instead of simultaneous because of prior knowledge while low-experience learners are at a disadvantage.

- Chunking principle

  In contrast to the contiguity principle, chunking recommends alternate or successive presentation of verbal and visual data although in short sections, not long ones. The main reason is the memory capacity. The concern is that an overload in working memory may ensue for having to carry huge chunks of information prior to establishment of connections. A study involving lightning storms validated the veracity of this principle where the participants that used the successive style displayed superior problem solving ability.

4. Emotion in Human–Computer Interaction. Emotion used to be persona non grata in the field of computer design. It had no place in the efficiency and rationality of computers which were the personification of zero emotion. Recent study findings in the field of psychology and technology show in a totally different light the relationship between humans, computers, and emotions.

Emotion has ceased to be considered only in light of anger generated by inexplicable computer crashes or hyper excitement caused by video games. Nowadays, it is widely accepted that a host of emotions are important part of computer-related activities such as Web search, sending an email, online shopping, and playing computer games. In almost everything now, the emotional systems get engaged according to psychologists.

Studies and discussions on emotion and computers have grown a lot because of dramatic advances in technology. Computers have actually been used to evaluate the relationship between emotion and its correlates. In the same vein, the astounding improvements in quality and speed of signal processing now enable computers to form conclusion on a user's emotional condition. Compared to purely textual interfaces that have very limited range, the multimodal interfaces that can use voices, faces, and bodies are now more capable of a broader range of emotions.

Nowadays, the performance of an interface will be seriously impeded without considering the user's emotional state. Surprisingly, it can earn even descriptions like socially inept, incompetent, and cold. Much remains to be done to successfully incorporate emotion recognition into interfaces. Still, more studies about the interaction between design and testing can help create interfaces that are efficient and effective while providing satisfaction and enjoyment.

When it comes to emotion, experts recommend that HCI interface designers focus on the basic ones first. Basic emotions are the same across cultures and designs that address this aspect has the largest potential beneficiaries or users. It is also easy to categorize or classify so manipulating or applying it in actual designs would be simple. The other side of focusing on it particularly in research is that not much is known at this point especially in the field of HCI how these basic emotions influence behaviors and attitudes. Studies in this field would surely lead to more opportunities. If an interface is considered as a medium and not simply a tool, then the emotional not just basic needs must be considered. The increasing popularity of catchwords like edutainment and infotainment reflects such a trend.

A degree of accuracy is necessary, however, in deducing emotions before an emotion-based design becomes plausible. There is a need to know more before an interface can tangle with human emotions. Also, there are sensitive boundaries that must be observed in monitoring human emotions and behaviors. Manipulating people is clearly a no no. Software designers must be aware of matters where consumers approve of emotion monitoring and adapting and incentives are always available. Finally, there is another role for computers in the area of human emotion: that of mediating face-to-face interactions between humans that promote effective communication.

5. Cognitive Architecture. A cognitive architecture is a computer simulation program that makes use of human cognition principle based on human experimental data. It also refers to software artifacts developed by computer programmers. Likewise, the term also includes large software systems which are considered hard to develop and maintain.

Right now, cognitive architectures are not widely utilized by HCI practitioners. Nevertheless, it is quite relevant as an engineering field to usability and has important applications in computing systems especially in HCI. It also serves as theoretical science in human computer interaction studies. Finally, cognitive architectures combine artificial intelligence methods and knowledge with data and principles from cognitive psychology.

Presently-known cognitive architectures are undergoing improvements and are being utilized in HCI-related tasks. Two of the most well-known systems, EPIC and ACT, are production systems or built around one. All systems have production rules which differ from architecture to architecture. The difference lies on focus and history although there's a certain similarity in intellectual history. They may have more congruence than differences at some levels either because of mutual borrowings or due to the convergence of the science. The third system, Soar, is a bit different than the first two production system models.

The three production systems, Soar, Epic, and ACT-R were developed to present different types of human cognition but showed more similarities than divergence as they developed. It is not easy to describe a value possessed by architecture as advantage because to others it constitutes a disadvantage. For instance, Soar's learning mechanism is very important for modeling the improvement of users for a period of time. But there are many applications also where Soar's features result to harmful side effects that can cause more difficulty in model construction.

6. <u>Task Loading and Stress in HCI</u>. Stress in the form of task loading is central to HCI. The traditional perspective on stress sees it in light of exposure to some adverse environmental situations such as noise and the focus of attention centers on most affected physiological system. A new way of looking at it, however, stems from the findings that all stress effects are mediated through the brain.

And since the brain is mainly focused on ongoing behavior or current task, stress ceases to be a peripheral issue but that the ongoing task becomes the primary source of stress. And this renders stress concerns that are central to all HCI issues. This means computer-based systems which aim at helping people lessen cognitive workload and task complexity actually impose more burdens and stress on them.

The person's coping mechanism for such stress affects their work performance and personal wellbeing. The environment may vary but some mechanisms for appraising stress in all task demands are the same. So for HCI, certain principles and designs for stress are applicable across multiple domains.

There are several theories of stress and performance and their connection to human-computer interaction. Workload and stress are at times considered as varying perspectives on the same problem. There are some general practices for stress mitigation. But quite important for this topic is setting up effective measures of information processing and mental resources. It also includes expounding on task dimensions that are relevant and their relationship to self-regulatory mechanisms.

It is critical to establish how an individual's appraisal of his/her environment can be influenced by personal traits and states. This is because stress can only be understood vis-a-vis interaction between a person and the environment. Lastly, it is better to treat stress at multiple levels whether physiological or organizational when making practical application. Instead of one-dimensional which is bound to fail, multidimensional is better as it considers the person, task, and the physical, social and organizational environments.

The implication is that HCI researchers and practitioners should go beyond the design of interface displays and controls and focus also on the person aspects. What are the things in the individual that affect performance and the physical-social environment where the human-technology interaction happens? It means that the technical principles at work in that situation are not adequate. They cannot develop a complete description of the relationship between resources and cognitive activities.

7. Motivating, Influencing, and Persuading Users. From its former role as tool for scientists, the spread of computer use to all sectors of society has brought new uses for computers. Among those uses are persuading people to change their attitudes and behavior. Nowadays, it is widely accepted that skills in motivating and persuading people are necessary for developing a successful HCI.

Interaction designers are actually agents of influence which unfortunately they have not yet understood and applied. Yet their works often involve creating something that tries to change people though they may not be conscious of it. Among these works are motivating people to register the software, learn an online application, or have product loyalty. Changing people's attitudes is now a common feature in the success of interactive products.

Depending on the types of product, the persuasion factor can either be small or large. At any rate, anything that needs to be marketed needs to be persuasive. The growing use of computing products and the limitless scalability of software makes interaction designers one of the best potential change agents in the future.

Take for example the Web-interaction designers who increasingly are facing more challenge in designing something that will hold the attention and motivation of information seekers. After that, they need to persuade web users to adopt certain behaviors like:
- using a software
- joining a survey
- clicking on the ads
- returning often after bookmarking a site
- buying things online
- releasing personal information
- forming an online community

Being able to persuade people is a measure of success here. But with success comes responsibility. The Web designer needs to make the website credible. The following are some broad guidelines to ensure credibility:

1. Design websites to present the real and practical aspects of the organization.
2. Invest sufficiently in visual design
3. Make websites that people can easily use.
4. Include markers of good quality
5. Use markers of reliability.
6. Avoid too much commercialism on a website
7. Adopt and adjust to the user experience
8. Avoid being amateurish

To sum it all, computer systems have become an inescapable part of everyday life. The interactive experience involving all systems be it mobile phone or desktop can be designed in such a way as to influence the way we think and act. By combining the computing capability with persuasion psychology, computer systems can motivate and persuade. Humans are undoubtedly still superior when it comes to influencing people. But in many areas of endeavor, computer can do what humans cannot even imagine being capable of.

Computers don't sleep and can be designed to keep trying on and on. At the very least, computers provide a new way for modifying how people act and think. Like it or not, the community of HCI professionals is at the forefront of the campaign to make more sensitive and responsive tech products. It can rise to the challenge of helping churn out products that enhance the people's over-all quality of life. Or it can continue being a tool to produce mindless products whose main reason for being into is to make profit for the owners.

## Fourth wave in interactive technology

The developments in computer technology and the accompanying changes in capabilities and functions came in several waves:

- First wave. At first, influence was not a part of the computer agenda. Fifty years ago, making computer devices workable and incrementally increasing its capabilities were the basic objective. Computer professionals were focused on function. That original focus continues until now.

- Second wave. This wave started in the 1970s as digital gaming like Atari appeared on the scene. The trend exploded. Second wave is mainly about entertainment and the momentum generated by computer-originated fun has not abated and has infected the world over creating a constantly growing multibillion dollar industry.

18

- Third wave. The 1980s saw the arrival of this wave. In this trend, ordinary people became the target of computer designers, human aspects specialists, and psychologists. It is mainly business because it is mass market expansion. But the trend focused on ease of use. The Apple Macintosh is the poster product of this trend having blazed the path to make computer use much easier. These three trends are continuing to roll even now. The third wave is foundational for HCI work actually.

- Fourth wave. Computers with persuasion functions appeared. In the 1970s and 1980s, some computer systems were developed for encouraging labor productivity and good health behaviors. But the advent of the Internet in late 1990 spurred more people to engage wholesale in creating interactive systems that can motivate and influence humans. There has been an unprecedented technological growth with strong persuasion component focusing on the end-user. The fourth wave, however, builds on the first three waves and could be as epochal.

## Functional Triad

The computer basically functions as social actor, media, and tool. People react to or view computers through any of these categories. They are also basic examples of experiences influencing and motivating people. These three categories are fleshed out under the Functional Triad framework. The tool function actually pertains to the way a computer seems to give power or new expertise to users. With the device, people are able to do things they were unable to accomplish in the past or do it an easier way at least.

The second function is that of media which has expanded vastly in the 1990s as the internet came of age and as graphics display and the information exchange capacity increased dramatically. The computer as medium can effectively send like no other sensory tools such things as live video or symbolic contents like text. Lastly, being social actors emanates from the fact that relationships have been formed by people with technologies.

Users are advised to respond socially when computers assume the following stance:

- adopt social mannerisms like greeting and apologizing

- practice animate functions like being an opponent, pet or coach.

- display animate features like emotions or physical characteristics

These three roles form the core of the Functional Triad leading to one interactive technology that makes for a total user experience. The Triad helps shed light on how computers can, through varying techniques, change behaviors and attitudes. There is a variation in impact according to which function is working. For instance, as social actor, the computer will persuade in a different manner than either as tool or media. Each role follows a different set of theories and strategies.

Computer as tools

Computers persuade as tools through:

a. process simplification
b. tailored information provision
c. more personal effectiveness
d. spurring decision-making

Computers are able to enhance self-efficacy, a key player in the process of changing behavior and attitude. Self-efficacy denotes confidence in one's ability to perform to succeed in a given aspect. The perception of great self-efficacy boosts one's confidence in taking action. Thus for individuals, computer systems can motivate them to be productive and efficient. An example is the computerized heart rate monitor. The monitor can lead people to believe they are achieving their exercise goals through heart rate data and burned calories.

The computer system in the monitor makes the task of monitoring calorie calculation and pulse taking easier. This increases the likelihood of a person continuing to exercise. When computers tailor information, they provide people contents that are relevant to their needs and situation. This encourages people to change their behavior and attitude.

Computers that spur technology in decision-making

It can also influence people by triggering a decision-making process. For example, today's web browsers launch a new window to alert people before they send information over insecure network connections. The message window serves as a signal to consumers to rethink their planned actions. A similar example exists in a very different context. Cities concerned with automobile speeding in neighborhoods can use a stand-alone radar trailer that senses the velocity of an oncoming automobile and displays that speed on a large screen. This technology is designed to trigger a decision-making process regarding driving speed.

Computers that guide people through a process by facilitating or simplifying a system for users and technology can minimize barriers that may impede a target behavior. For example, in the context of web commerce, technology can simplify a multi-step process down to a few mouse clicks. Typically, in order to purchase something online, a consumer needs to select an item, place it in a virtual shopping cart, proceed to checkout, enter personal and billing information, and verify an order confirmation. Amazon.com and other e-commerce companies have simplified this process by storing customer information so that consumers need not reenter information for every transaction.

8. Human-Error Identification in Human–Computer Interaction. The leap from focusing on human error in technological problems to a less obvious culprit started in the 1940's. It was established during that year that plane pilot error was often designer error. It began to show that design is the key to substantially reduce human error and this paradigm continued to gather steam particularly in HCI.

It is now common wisdom that human error can be as often as the product of a defective design or as a person making a mistake. The inadequate design fosters activities that lead to errors. A groundbreaking outcome of this new philosophy is that errors are now viewed as totally predictable events instead of seeing it as unpredictable occurrences. This makes errors avoidable.

So errors became instances where planned series of steps and activities fail to realize intended results independent of any outside change agencies. If errors are no longer random, then it can be identified and predicted ahead of time. What partially drove this line of thinking are the accidents that happened in the nuclear industry that is hungry for preemptive solutions. This has led to the formulation of several human-error identification (HEI) techniques.

Although evaluative and summative in nature, these HEI techniques that employ ergonomics methods can now be used in formative design stages especially in analytic prototyping. For instance, the entry of computer-aided design such as in architecture has profound impacts on prototyping. It made possible what was considered as impossible or too prohibitively costly design alteration at the structural prototyping stage.

The three main forms of prototyping human interfaces have been identified namely: functional analysis, scenario analysis, and structural analysis.

Functional analysis includes consideration of the functional range supported by the device. In comparison, scenario analysis is exemplified by consideration of the device in relation to events sequence. An example of the structural analysis, on the other hand, is the use of user-centered viewpoint in a non-destructive testing of the interface.

One compelling example of the crucial role of design in predicting and minimizing errors concern human error identification (HEI) tools like the TAFEI or Task Analysis for Error Identification. The results of the application of TAFEI on interface project designs show how it can improve systems and its relevance to other ergonomic methods. It served to validate what has been long suspected when it comes to error-design relationship as follow:

- Structured systems like TAFEI results to reliable and trustworthy error data;

- Most errors resulting from technology are totally predictable;

- To improve design and reduce errors, ergonomics methods should be employed in formative design process.

Exploring design weaknesses through tools like TAFEI will go a long way in developing and producing devices and gadgets that are tolerant to error.

## Classifying human error

A classification framework for human errors is helping in anticipating and analyzing error. This has been made possible by the formulation of a system for error prediction. Error analysis makes use of psychological aspects and taxonomic scheme. One category is mode error which needs special focus in designing HCI systems. Input mistakes due to erroneous classification of system mode could have very adverse results. Consequences may include document loss for word processing; recording loss for videos; and aircraft damage for flight decks. The people responsible for design need to thoroughly understand human error.

Systems for classifying require proven techniques for predicting errors based on a design scheme that factor in the requirements of users. A more complex way of classifying errors includes mistakes, lapses, and slips. Memory malfunction is at the root of lapses while attention breakdown attends slips. Lapses and slips are categorized under unintentional action while mistakes fall under actions that are intended. These error types are quite useful in identifying human errors in HCI.

The following are the identified categories of errors:

❖ **Error in description** - specifying intention is not complete or unclear

❖ **Mode errors** - classifying situation is incorrect

❖ **Errors driven by data** - outside events that triggered schema activation

❖ **Errors of failing to activate** – trigger point fails in schema activation

❖ **Capture errors** - stronger sequence prevails in action sequences that are the same

❖ **Errors in activating association** - schemas that are active and which also activate fellow schemas associated with them

❖ **Errors in loss of activation** - after being activated these schemas lose activation

❖ **Errors in activating prematurely** - activation of schemas happens too soon

❖ **Blend errors** - component mixture from competing schemas

An example of mode errors is the raising of landing gear by a pilot when the plane is still running on the runway. The error stemmed from faulty system design that causes confusion and unsuitable mode operation. A sample solution would then be configuring the landing gear to sense the weight it carries while still on the ground to incapacitate the relevant switch. Every activity is subject to mistake, lapse or a slip so the classification scheme helps in anticipating any aberration that could happen in a task

### Human error prediction

No doubt, it would be revolutionary if human errors can be safely predicted. Still, two main problems have been identified in current human error identification techniques. One is the failure to factor in what the gadget in question is doing in HCI including the context. Another is the tendency to depend entirely on the judgment of the analyst. Problems arise when various analysts with divergent experiences give different predictions on the same issue. Or an analyst gives differing conclusions at different times. The subjectivity poses a stumbling block to prediction reliability. Expertise in technique and in operating the device in question is essential for the analyst.

To overcome these hurdles, two techniques were developed for predicting errors as follow:

1. Systematic Human Error Reduction and Prediction Approach or SHERPA makes use of a different method for predicting error. It uses as much as ten error modes in associating with an activity or action. An inexperienced analyst, however, might give an excessive number of predictions just to be safe.

2. Task Analysis For Error Identification or TAFEI, on the other hand, works in a different way. It functions by pinpointing potential conversions between various conditions of a device and utilizes the behavioral description from the Hierarchical Task Analysis or HTA to classify possible errors. A noteworthy advantage over SHERPA is that it does not appear to lead to a surfeit of false alarms even with an

inexperienced analyst. Limiting TAFEI use to the conversions between gadget conditions prevents unnecessary prediction of errors. SHERPA is essentially mostly dependent on the analyst's judgment for determining which error modes are suitable for each task stage. The use of the HTA emanates from the idea that the goals, operations, and plans can represent the performance of tasks.

Goals here, of course, refer to what is intended achievement, operations pertain to steps done to fulfill goals, and plans are about the order by which operations are done. SHERPA's objective is not merely knowing an existing design's possible error but likewise providing guidance to design aspects in the future. The nature of analysis procedure is helpful for solving problems which can lead to many improvements. It overlooks, however, various solutions that can obviate programming.

For the TAFEI, another distinct feature is its adherence to an approach based on schema. There is a clear-cut goal to assess human-machine interaction. It is done by matching the conditions of the machine with the activities of users. TAFEI have three main features: the Transition Matrices or TM, the State-Space Diagrams or SSD, and HTA. TM enables the determination of possible errors as the device and user interact. SSDs help describe the actions of a machine and HTA or the human activity. Basically, TAFEI does it the following way:

- Define the system.

- Analyze separately the machine conditions and the human actions.

- Combine the two analyses to come up with TAFEI's representation of the interaction between machine and user.

There is a matrix of transitions where each transition is analyzed. The categories of transitions according to performance or results are:

❖ Legal which means transition is achievable and is error-free based on HTA description

❖ Illegal or transition is probable but cannot fulfill desired results; used to consider needed changes

❖ Impossible or transition is not possible

Like SHERPA, TAFEI's analysis scheme aims to provide guidance to designing activities for the purpose of making products tolerant to errors.

**Confirming identification of human error**

Both SHERPA and TAFEI appear to show a sufficient sensitivity level in error prediction. It is comparable to another predictive scheme, the Cognitive Reliability and Error Analysis Method or CREAM which records a 68.6% fit for both actual and predicted results. The HEI techniques allow experts a structured assessment. Other HEI schemes include the heuristic approach which requires a clear cut methodology for a structured assessment.

A better scheme is one with a semi-structured approach like the TAFEI and SHERPA that allows analysts to form judgment without posing hindrances. Analysts are spared the burden of excessive memory load while being able to employ their heuristic interpretations. TAFEI, in particular, is useful in the process of designing interface for computer workstations. In an assessment for medical imaging software, an error was identified showing the interface as not supportive of the pertinent events sequence.

Problems include too much number of steps in the sequence of tasks to be performed and the bewildering availability of options given to users in each system condition. SHERPA, however, achieved vindication when combined with expert judgment. It garnered top marks and showed impressive results making it the best approach to use. One factor for the excellent results is the high degree of ecological validity. The activity made adequate use of the expertise of expert analysts for error prediction.

The final verdict, however, would come in only after some methodological concerns have been thoroughly addressed. Not to be left behind, TAFEI also produced noteworthy reports. It had been instrumental in successful interface design completions and appears to support prototyping analytically. Designers are able to concentrate on the interface design, activities of the user, and sequence of tasks. More importantly, the use of TAFEI pinpoints possible areas where problems or errors may appear in the interaction. What makes such accomplishment more exemplary is the auditable, systematic, structured, and rigorous way TAFEI does it.

Similarly, SHERPA was employed in a study involving safety critical systems, in this case in oil extraction industries, partly to test its effectiveness. The findings shed light on some problems being experienced by the company. The SHERPA-based analysis yielded proposed solutions with solid implications on human-computer interface design such as:

- link the members of the drilling team electronically

- mud loss tables that are computer-generated

- separate displays for drilling parameters placement

- shutdown process that is automated

- automatic information transmission

- internet-based weather schemes

- computerized procedures

- alarm levels prompted by a computer, modify trend displays design

- probe of various drilling features as prompted by the computer

It was strongly recommended that the proposed solutions be adopted as they would lead to safer systems design and avoidance of devastating disasters.

# Chapter 3: The Computer Side in the HCI

The salient points when it comes to the computer side in HCI include:

1. <u>Input Technologies and Techniques.</u>  Input devices which are also a classification of computer can detect physical aspects of places, things, and, of course, people. However, its function is never complete without considering the visual feedback corresponding to the input. It is like using a writing instrument without something to write on. Input and output should always go together.

   And in devices with small screens, this is only possible with the help of integrated sensors. If the user or human characteristics are important in a maximized HCI environment, so are input technologies with enough sophistication to meet user-machine interaction requirements. Users can only achieve the task objectives by combining the right feedback with inputs. In this regard, the HCI designer should take into account the following:

   a. the industrial and ergonomic design of the gadget

   b. the physical censor

   c. the relationship among all interaction techniques

   Input gadgets have many properties that apply to the usual pointing devices or mobile items with touch input. These pointing devices include the: mice, trackballs, isometric joysticks, isotonic joysticks, indirect tablets, touchpads, touchscreens, and pen-operated devices. The mice or mouse, of course, is one of the most popular as anyone who has ever used a computer knows. Because of its inherent advantages for individual users where it can easily be used by most people, it is one of the most preferred pointing devices.

   Touchpads are most well-known to laptop users. These are small tablets that are sensitive to touch and which are usually featured on laptop units. Touchscreens on the other hand are tablets that are sensitive to touch which are placed on a display. It is increasingly becoming the tool to beat because of the proliferation of smart phones and other hand-held devices.

   There are input models and theories that are quite helpful in evaluating the efficacy of interaction strategies. But it would be most beneficial to readers here to focus on current and future trends for this feature. Interactive system designers should go beyond the usual things like graphical user interface and pointing ideas when it comes to inputs.

   They must delve deeper into more effective search strategies, sensor inputs for new data types, and techniques of synthesis to make much better sense of data. Better search tools will enhance navigation and manual search regarding file systems. One outstanding development is the breakthrough in the development of more advanced sensor inputs such as technologies for tagging and location.

It allows computers to identify physical objects and locations that have been tagged, and to detect their location and distance to other devices through signal strength analysis. These sensors are making interface personalization much easier. This development in interaction also has great implications for data mining and techniques for machine learning. Continuous improvement in structure synthesis and extraction techniques is invaluable in this data-rich era.

An overriding aim in HCI is to achieve dramatic advancement in humanity's interaction with technology. The computer side of this presents limitless possibilities but the cognitive skills and senses of man will be relatively stagnant. Our holding, touching, and object-movement are not the result of technology-like progress but a product of our human limitations.

2.  Recognition- and Sensor-Based Input for Interaction. Computers are able to manipulate physical signals that have been transformed by sensors into electrical signals. Sensors have found their way into various fields of industry such as robotics, automotive, and aerospace. It has also found vast applications in consumer products.

The computer mouse is a very good example. Imagine that simple-looking device equipped with algorithms that process images and specialized camera that enables it to be unbelievably sensitive to motions. It detects movement at the rate of a thousand of an inch several thousand times per second. Another interesting device is the accelerometer that detects acceleration due to movement and continuous acceleration because of gravity.

Digital cameras now make use of accelerometers to save a photo. Laptops also are equipped with accelerometers for self-protection. When the laptop is accidentally dropped the accelerometer enables the hard disk to secure the hard drive prior to impact. With smartphones, the goal is for motion sensing for the purpose of interaction such as determining the walking pattern of users. Generally, HCI research on sensors dwells on its usage to improve interaction.

Sensor studies are either to broaden input options or build new computing forms. The new forms include mobile devices that recognize locations and places that are sensitive to the presence and needs of its inhabitants. Still there are far more advanced goals and applications like in robotics.

There is a race to develop machines that will behave and think like humans or at least complement their capabilities. It has many critical applications such as in nuclear power accident mitigation. One worry, of course, is that it will end up in the military. But in safety, mobile computing, entertainment, productivity, affective computing, and surveillance, sensors are finding widespread application.

An intriguing side note here is the idea of developing a sensor to enable computers to detect and accordingly react to the frustration of its user. The computer's response could be something like playing relaxing music. Sensing could be in the form of the user banging on the keyboard in frustration. A microphone could react to the yelling of the speaker or the webcam could sense scowling.

In general, the potential of interactive sensing is quite good. The degree of progress across the whole computing spectrum actually gives the impression that sky is the limit. Advances in nanotechnology, CPU power, and storage capacities will continue to produce more outstanding innovations in the computer side of HCI.

But what is driving the unprecedented growth of the sensor-based interactive systems is the dizzying expansion in devices outside the old desktop computer. It is hard to keep track of the explosive proliferation of smart phones, tablet PCs, portable gaming devices, music and movie players, living room-centric computers, and personal digital assistants. Computing is becoming part and parcel of our daily life and our environment.

Through recognition techniques and sensing systems, task-specific computing devices will be developed instead of general functions. It will also pave the way for different types of interaction style in HCI. This activity-specific interactive systems development will further hasten innovations on a much broader array of practical applications.

3. Visual Displays. Timekeeping has always been one function that man has strived for a good visual display. Today's smartwatches which are actually wrist computers sport stunning visual displays. It is no longer limited to displaying time but is multifunctional. Some brands can pinpoint exact location in the planet through a global positioning system. Others can show heart rate while a number can be personal digital assistants.

The main idea behind wearable computing is that the human body is wearing the visual displays. One major way people use wearables is to put the display on one's head making user's hands free to work. It is called headmounted displays or HMDs. The screen-based is one category of HMDs. It makes use of the retinal-projection method which projects images on the retina of the eye.

29

An alternative method is the scanning displays which scan images onto the retina pixel by pixel. A second type of display which is actually much bigger in scope and the most widespread is the hand-held and wrist-worn displays. They are in mobile phones, media players, wristwatches, and other portable gadgets. Apple is one of the global leaders in this field and the most well-known. Even textiles for clothing are now being used for such technology in what is now known as photonic textiles-fabric.

Multicolored lighting systems were merged with the fabrics for its electronic information function without affecting the cloth's softness. It has sensors, GSM, and Bluetooth! Photonic fabrics have great promising applications in the areas of personal health care and communication.

### Human-Related Display Criteria

Visual displays for wearables are worn by people. A very popular type of these wearables is the HMDs or the head-mounted displays. The main idea is to enable the user to work hands-free. There are three classifications of HMDs, namely:

- **screen-based** – HMDs in which the elements of pictures are formed in a spatially adjacent manner.

- **ocular image forming displays** – rely on technologies like digital mirror devices (DMD), LCD, CRT, and organic light-emitting diodes (OLEDS).

- **scanning displays** – pixel by pixel scanning of image onto the retina directly and is an option in place of screen-based displays

Most HMDs in circulation are based on transmissive displays. Also, it is possible to combine the screen-based technology with scanning system. The HMDs can also be classified based on functionality: binocular, biocular, and monocular. Monocular displays are for one eye only and, hence, lighter compared to the other two. But all three types can give the image in see-through style.

Apart from HMDs, the other classifications of displays are the hand-held and the wrist worn. These other types have become ubiquitous around the world because they have been incorporated into media players, mobile phones, wristwatches, PDA or personal digital assistants, and other mobile gadgets.

4. Haptic Interfaces. Haptic interface refers to a device for sending feedback that produces sensation of weight, touch, rigidity, and other aspects through the skin and muscle. This force feedback mechanism is designed to enhance computer-human interaction. Because haptics are done through actual

physical contact, they are not easy to synthesize unlike the sense of sight and sound that are gathered through the eyes and ears.

The genius in the haptic interface is that it simply makes use of the body's own highly sophisticated receptor system. The haptic feedback is made possible through synthetic stimulation in the skin and proprioception.

Proprioception involves something deeper than the skin – the muscle and skeleton. The mechanoreceptors in the body enable its detection of contact forces received from the environment. Body receptors sense velocity, skin stretching, vibration, and edges of objects. Haptic interfaces are more widely applied in the field of virtual reality than in information media and related devices are now available commercially.

Two of the most important research needs on haptic interfaces in the future concern the psychology in haptics and safety considerations. Safety is a crucial issue as insufficient actuator control can lead to injuries for users. Control problems may occur with the tool displays and exoskeleton. Unintended forces or vibration may pose danger to the user.

A locomotion interface that holds a user's body can cause serious physical damage if control is inadequate. It requires proven safety equipment that amply protects the walker and this should be a major objective of research. A much safer alternative is a system where the user does not wear any equipment during the interaction.

The psychology in haptics on the other hand requires more studies on muscle sensation as most existing findings are on skin sensation. Among the few promising findings relate to Laderman and Klatzky's work (1987) on force display and their recent study of forces distributed according to space. Their psychological findings have very promising applications in the development of haptic interface. A lot of obstacles need to be overcome before usage of haptic interface becomes widespread.

Though men cannot do without haptics in real life interaction, it is still of limited use in HCI. One can say haptic interface is still in infancy with its 10-year background. So eventually its time will come just like image displays (e.g. TV and movies) which started 100 years ago. For now, what are available are a few haptic interfaces with limited functionality and high cost. At the very least, haptic interface is a new very promising frontier in HCI with immense potential contribution to man's quality of life.

5. <u>Non-speech Auditory Output</u>. Sound is one of the key aspects that complete our interaction with our environment. But where speech is direct and necessitates focus and attention, non-speech sound is more diffused and provides a different class of information.

Non-speech sounds include sounds from the environment, music, and sound effects. Nevertheless, speech and non-speech sounds complement each other just like text is complemented by visual symbols. Non-speech sounds can give information in a shorter period of time than speech.

Right now, the non-speech field needs more research. The user interface is a much more effective tool for HCI when it employs a combined visual and sound feedback. This sound-visual combination has complementary function as well. Visual gives specific information about a small area reached by our eyes but sound or the auditory system provides more general information from beyond our focus.

Our senses are the key to our effective interaction with the external world. These senses in turn bring more dimensions in information as they enhance one another. These principles are very useful in a multimodal HCI by adding non-speech sound output to the graphical displays. An example of this application is focusing our eyes on one task like editing a manuscript while monitoring other aspects in the machine through sound.

Reliance on visual sense which is more prevalent at present can be problematic. One problem is there could be visual overload which means the user could miss lots of information. Or simply that the viewer cannot look at everything at the same time at all times. Sound can help eliminate that situation by giving information to the user that the eyes could not see.

This interdependence between visual and audio could make information presentation far more efficient. Non-speech sound is mainly used in games' sound effects, music, and other multimedia usages. It is commonly employed in creating a certain mood for the item like in movies. In HCI, sound is used to provide information particularly those things that a user does not see or notice such as what is going on in their computer systems.

It is useful to use non-speech sound in HCI for many reasons. Seeing and hearing in the human body is first of all interdependent. The eyes can give information that is high-resolution only in a limited area of focus. But sounds can be received from all sides of the user: front, above, below, and behind. This not only provides direct information but also tells the eyes where to look to get more useful data. In fact, at times reaction to sound stimuli is faster than what is seen.

Non-speech sound can therefore help in reducing large display overload which can cause users to miss important data. This is especially true in large graphical interfaces that use multiple monitors. Using sound to present some information would reduce screen space. It would also lessen the volume of information that should be on the screen. This is most relevant to gadgets with small visual displays like smartphones and PDAs.

Non-speech sound would also decrease demands on our visual attention. For instance, a user who is walking would miss much information as he looks at his device's visual display because of competing attention from the traffic or uneven surface where he is walking. In fact, if the information is in sound, he does not have to look at his device at all.

Our sense of sound is also underutilized. Yet as exemplified by classical music, its intricate organization can make, say a symphony, a powerful tool for transmitting complex information. The beauty with sound is that it grabs attention. It is easy to avoid looking at something but hard to ignore sound which makes it very effective in sending important information. Likewise, certain things in the interface look more natural in sound than in sight.

Finally, non-speech sound will allow visually-impaired users to use computers. Newer graphical displays have, in particular, made it even harder for them to operate the device. Research has been extensive in the HCI application of non-speech sound in a wide range of topics.

There are two main areas of growth where the application of non-speech sound has the best potential. One is in the creation of multimodal displays that utilizes all available senses. This means integrating sound with other things like force-feedback and tactile apart from sight. The other area is in wearable and mobile computing gadgets that also use multimodal displays. As mentioned, the screens of these devices are small and sound will reduce the need for screen space.

6. <u>Network-Based Interaction</u>. Networked interfaces have modified our perception of society and the world at large particularly with the Web and now mobile devices. There are several roles that networks play in HCI. The first is as an Enabler which refers to things that can be done only with network. The second is as Mediator which pertains to problems and issues caused by networks.

Third is as Subject which focuses on managing and understanding networks and fourth as Platform which dwells on interface architectures and algorithms. Network includes both the wire-based and the wireless world. Things are rapidly changing especially in the wireless networks. These changes can be classified in two dimensions, namely:

- **Global vs. Local** – refers to the distance by space between the connected points such as machines in the office to global networks like the Internet.

- **Fixed vs. Flexible** – pertains to the nature of the links between points such as fixed devices and gadget that configures itself. More changes are coming because of spreading wireless links. One example is being able to gain access to internet connections and printers of another office by simply plugging a portable device into the Ethernet.

Traditionally, LANs belong to local-fixed category while Internet is global-fixed. Hand-helds like cell phones are also categorized as global-fixed because phones are fixed and independent of location. The internet makes use of domain names which are fixed like URLs. Some phone technologies like GSM and GPRS are classified as global-fixed because it is possible to send content that is based on location. Also the enlarging data capability is enabling services to handle huge media content.

What set these technologies apart, however, are the connectivity model and the charging which are usually by data use or fixed charge. There are a number of current and new technologies from the local-flexible type. These include the Wi-Fi, infrared, Bluetooth, and ZigBee which permit flexible connections among personal gadgets. With them, a computer device can utilize a mobile-phone modem or a headset with Bluetooth can make connections with a phone, wireless. Unfortunately, these capabilities also enhance unsavory activities like illegal equipment accessing, hacking, and surveillance.

7. <u>Wearable Computers</u>. Computers have become like appendage to many office workers. But it is hard for those using mobile devices to get the information they need. In a mobile situation, existing interfaces will hamper the user's main task. Users will be forced to prioritize the device instead of the environment. The need is for a wearables design that helps fulfill not obstruct the task.

A framework that can be very useful in creating good designs of computer interfaces which are wearable is CAMP. This framework addresses different factors that may impinge on the effectiveness of the design such as body closeness and how it is used. CAMP stands for:

- <u>Corporal</u> – which means absence of discomfort to users during physical interface with the wearable.
- <u>Attention</u> – interface design should allow user to focus both on the real world and virtual reality.
- <u>Manipulation</u> – there are adequate controls which are easy to manipulate particularly in a mobile environment.
- <u>Perception</u> – Design must enable user to quickly perceive displays even when mobile. So displays should be easy to navigate and simple.

Outside offices and buildings, an attractive option for a user to have access to a computer interface is through wearables. There are challenges however that need to be addressed to fulfill the tasks in terms of contextual awareness, interface, adaptation to tasks, and cognitive model. These include:

- **Modalities of Input/output** – the ease of use and accuracy of modalities developed that try to copy the human brain's input/output capacity are not yet satisfactory. Frustrations bedevil users when there are inaccuracies. Also the computing requirement of these modalities is way beyond what low-weight wearable devices have. Input devices which are simple to use are needed.

- **Models of User interface** – there is a need for extensive experimentation in using applications involving end-users.

- **Capability-applications matching** – evaluation and design of interface should prioritize development of most effective way to access information and avoid creating additional features.

- **Simple methodology in interface evaluation** – current evaluation approaches are too complicated and time-consuming making them unsuitable in interface design. What is needed is an evaluation methodology that addresses frustration and human errors.

- **Context awareness** – for context aware computing to be realized, several questions must be answered. These include application models that integrate the social and cognitive aspects, social and cognitive mapping of inputs from many sensors, anticipating the needs of users, and interacting with the users.

9. Workstation Design for Computers. Although fixed computer set ups are still a sizeable part of workstation design, it has been overtaken by portable information technologies which are not fixed. The use of these highly mobile gadgets is now so widespread involving many areas of human endeavors. And they are also quite removed from how traditional fixed work stations work. With the proliferation of these portable information devices (PIDs), ergonomic concerns have cropped up with regards work area designs.

Not much work has been done in establishing parameters for designing PIDs work areas. Ergonomics refers to the science of matching the needs and capacities of people with the activities and environment. Based on ergonomic principles, work set up is adjusted based on a person's social, psychological, and physical conditions.

## a. Ergonomics principles

Ergonomics aims to enhance both performance and work environment such as safety, health, and comfort. Better computer interfaces and suitable furnitures are not the only concern. Design principles must also include the social and environmental aspects as well as specific needs of the job. It is essential for good ergonomics to minimize the pressure on the joints and back of the user to maintain good body posture. It must also reduce repetitious movement of any body part as well as period of non-movement while affording enough rest or work breaks.

Four decades ago, the average workplace using the simple typewriter enabled a worker to move around and interact with others. But with the advent of computers, a lot of people started staying seated with their computer most of their working hours. This kind of human-computer interaction where people are mostly in sedentary situation has caused innumerable health problems. In addition, the massive improvements in technology have created a multifaceted environment that brought people working not only in fixed position but also in mobile situations.

Although movement is good for the body, it also introduced functional problems in the use of devices such as in the area of perceptual-motor capabilities. In general, poor ergonomic designs are reportedly causing pain and discomfort in muscles and skeletons, visual problems, and even psychological issues. The effectiveness of both technology and user is affected by the condition of each one. The state of the environment, task requisites, the workstation, and work requirements will determine how effective one can use the technology.

Conversely, the status of the user in terms of things like readiness and health will impact how effective the technology will be. As a result, the quality of human-computer interaction also depends heavily on the workspace design. Cramped spaces, for example, that limit physical movement can cause debilitating postures leading to health problems that hinder performance. Nowadays, mobile computing has become in vogue and users use their devices in any area where they are in. And the probability of ergonomic mishaps for these kind of technology could well be substantial also.

## b. Design considerations for fixed workstations.

Minimizing musculoskeletal complications and enhancing comfort of users are some of the key design aspects for workstations. This includes things like the design of the input devices, screen, and even making hard copies. Some of the work conditions that contribute to posture and musculoskeletal problems are:

- presence of glare and inadequate lighting

- cramped working space

- posture where the arms, trunk, and neck are unmoving

- available avenue for movement are awkward and unnatural

- seats are not designed for good shoulder and back position

- keyboards are on uneven surfaces

- the space available for the toe and knee is not enough

- chairs that are not sufficiently padded in the seat and backrest, inadequate arm rests, and non-adjustable height for seat pan

As a result, the following recommendations have been given by ergonomics experts:

➢ enough space for the knees are needed for seated users

➢ keyboards on the surface of the desk should be movable

➢ furnitures should be able to adjust to the type of body and movement of users.

➢ adjustment mechanisms for workstations must be user- friendly

➢ together with a feature for supporting the lumbar, the backrest of the chair must be long enough and the incline adjustable.

The compilation of findings from many studies incorporating all validated recommendations on the subject produced the following guidelines for designing fixed workstation:

✓ the position of source documents should enable proper body posture specifically the alignment of the back and upper extremities as well as comfortable viewing for the users.

✓ more working areas as needed for writing on, layouting, reading, storing, as well as handling materials, technologies like PIDs, and documents

✓ the distance for viewing must be comfortable enough for different people through a display screen that can be positioned farther or nearer

✓ table must be high enough to afford a comfortable level for input devices like the mouse and sufficient space for the knee and thigh (51 cm minimum width for leg space, 60 cm and 38 cm minimum depths respectively from toe level and from knee level; 60 cm to 80 cm range of adjustment for single adjustable table height, 59 cm to 71 cm from keyboard, and 90 cm to 115 cm from screen for independently adjustable table height)

✓ in several points in working area or surface, there should be a detachable mouse and detachable keyboard

✓ more thigh and knee space through thinner table top

✓ enough legroom for necessary movements or position adjustments in the course of work.

An excellent design for a computer workstation takes into consideration different body sizes and even goes beyond minimum measures for better posture and movement. Table heights, for instance, should depend on the height of the man.

c. **Workstation design for laptops**

Laptops have proliferated in the planet with some social development-conscious manufacturers trying to develop a cheap version to help Third World have-nots. Laptop is quite portable so you can work and play with your computer anywhere. For the office worker, you can bring your work at home or anywhere outside the office where you can do presentations. All files that normally need a file cabinet can be brought anywhere. This proliferation of laptops has prompted the International Ergonomics Association (IEA) through its Human–Computer Interaction Committee to issue the following ergonomic guidelines for work environment and workstation design:

• *Environment for work and work station design.* Design a environment that is suited for your work

1. Good environment for using the laptop includes proper temperature and lighting. The place should neither be too lighted or dark.

2. Have a desk surface with sufficient space for the laptop

• *Desk and Chair.* The height of the chair should fit your physique.

1. The height of the chair should be adjusted in accordance with the keyboard height with forearm parallel with keyboard.

2. Use a footrest if feet are not long enough to stand flat on floor area.

3. Adequate space must be available under the desk.

• *On keyboard.* Position keyboard in a good angle, using palm rest if needed.

1. Based on what is comfortable to you and your type of posture, modify the keyboard's angle.

2. Your wrists must be able to rest comfortably through enough space near the keyboard or on the desktop itself if keyboard is thin enough.

3. An external keyboard is recommended if keyboard is difficult to use.

- _Proper posture for working_. Avoid unnatural postures, and change your posture occasionally.

  1. Use the right posture. Do not be in a twisted posture or leaning too much backward or forward at extended periods.

  2. There should be at least a 40-50 cm distance from your eyes to the display. Being too near the display may cause eye strain.

  3. From time to time look at a farther distance 6 m at least to give the eyes rest and avoid eye fatigue.

  4. Ensure a natural angle for your wrists.

- _For input devices without keyboard_. For pointing purposes, utilize a mouse if possible.

  1. Whenever possible, use a mouse and a mouse pad.

  2. Know fully how to operate the internal pointing mechanism if the use of a mouse is not possible.

Although awesomely portable, situations for handhelds that are uncomfortable and ergonomically wrong are all too real. For instance in an airport where you want to finish some work while waiting for your flight. You decided to rent a kiosk with work desk, adjustable chair, privacy, and high speed computer. Still, the features of these workplaces are usually not up to the best ergonomic standards. A short time interacting with a computer device in such a situation for one hour may still be okay but extended periods will produce unwanted physical side effects.

It could be injury, pain, and discomfort in the skeleton and muscles. The reality is actually more severe. Rather than being in exclusive cubicles, a widespread scene often seen in major airports is that of many people seated in nonadjustable benches or chairs with inappropriate back support. They punch away on their laptops which are placed on their laps. Or it could be a hand-held device such as Ipad through which you can access the internet and use email or facebook. It is more portable than the laptop and can be used while seated near your gate for boarding or when lining up at the check-in counter.

One of its main drawbacks, of course, is the very small buttons that provide visual difficulties. The different unstructured and unregulated positions using the hand-held gadgets often cause harmful position for the shoulders, neck, back, wrists or hands, legs and other body parts. Also the extended use of the very small features such as keyboards or buttons that lead to bad posture can cause problems in the tendons, muscles, nerves, ligaments, and joints. It can result to painfulness in the muscle area as well. Devices that use audio and voice can put unwanted pressure on the ears, the voice, and the neck.

The following recommendations are made to overcome the poor ergonomic features of such workstations:

- With a laptop, look for a place where there is a table where you can put your laptop on instead of on your lap. Apply the laptop guidelines from EIA by arranging the area as similar as could be done.

- With a handheld gadget, protect your back by being in the right place usually in a sitting position unless you are walking. You can also use an earpiece or a headset with both microphone and earphone features to minimize the use of hands. Avoid overuse to prevent ear and voice problems and ensure recovery through frequent use interruptions.

- Avoid poor posture in working especially longer than 30 minutes. You can do 10 minute rests every so often, stand and do some stretching, or walk a bit. Or you can put away your device for a while and sit down or do some relaxing routines like being seated on the floor with your back on a wall or backrest.

- Get the best quality especially in ergonomic designs in terms of displays and interfaces such as typing pads, headphones, and screens. The demands for perceptual motor functioning are much bigger with the small devices. Screens, for instance, must show more readable contents and the buttons should be easily operated, preferably properly spaced and large.

- Utilize these small gadgets only when you have no choice such as having no access to larger workstations and only for a limited time.

### d. **On wearables, handhelds, and PIDs**

More ergonomic concerns are expected with these smaller portable devices. They are much harder to operate with both hands and the eyes due to the small displays. Design trends therefore are also focusing on haptic interfaces, sound, and verbal communications . Communicating with other devices is already part of the capabilities of some PIDs. Cell phones especially smart phones is the most prolific example of these PIDs. It is now all over the planet and its capabilities are astounding including audio streaming, photographing, emailing, recording, television, texting, and telephone calling. Yet it continues to shrink in size and with it the interfaces and displays. The first to be sacrificed in such a change is comfort and effectiveness in usage.

# Conclusion

Thank you again for purchasing this book!

I hope this book was able to help you to gain useful knowledge and understanding about human-computer interaction.

The next step is to apply what you have learned.

Finally, if you enjoyed this book, please take the time to share your thoughts and post a review on Amazon. It'd be greatly appreciated!

Thank you and good luck!

www.ingramcontent.com/pod-product-compliance
Lightning Source LLC
Chambersburg PA
CBHW060932050326
40689CB00013B/3057